ARIEL DORFMAN

Ariel Dorfman is considered one o ....ntieth century's most important literary voices, especially as a forceful example of cross-cultural writing. Dorfman, of Argentine-Chilean origin, details his life of exile and bicultural living in his acclaimed memoir, *Heading South, Looking North*.

Besides his work as a poet, novelist and essayist, Dorfman has built up an impressive body of work. His books have been translated into more than forty languages and performed in over 100 countries. His plays include *Death and the Maiden* (1991), which won the Olivier Award for Best Play, and was made into a film by Roman Polanski; *Widows* (1991, with Tony Kushner); and *Reader*, which opened at the Traverse Theatre as part of the Edinburgh Festival in 1995. He has written non-fiction as well, including *The Empire's Old Clothes* (1996), *Exorcising Terror* (2004) and *Other Septembers, Many Americas* (2005). He has won numerous international awards, including two from the Kennedy Center. In 1996, with his son, Rodrigo, he received an award for best television drama in Britain for *Prisoners in Time*. His poems, *Last Waltz in Santiago*, have been turned into a fiction film, *Deadline*, featuring the voices of Emma Thompson, Bono, Harold Pinter and others.

Dorfman's human-rights play, *Speak Truth to Power: Voices from Beyond the Dark* (based on interviews with human-rights defenders by Kerry Kennedy), premiered at the Kennedy Center in Washington in 2000, starring Kevin Kline, Sigourney Weaver, Alec Baldwin, John Malkovich, among others. It has gone on to many performances around the world, including a production in Martin Luther King's church in Atlanta, with Martin Sheen, Sean Penn, Robin Wright Penn and Woody Harrelson, among others.

His latest plays are *Purgatorio*, *The Other Side* and *Picasso's Closet*; and his most recent novels are *Blake's Therapy* and *Americanos: Los Pasos de Murieta*. He has also written a libretto for the musical *Dancing Shadows* (with Eric Woolfson, lead composer and singer of the Alan Parsons Project), which garnered five Tony Awards when it opened in Korea in 2007. He is also a regular contributor to major newspapers around the world. He is currently working on the second volume of his memoirs and a new opera based on a legend from the Upanishades, updated to address the global exploitation of children.

He holds the Walter Hines Page Chair of Literature and Latin American Studies at Duke University.

His website is www.adorfman.duke.edu

Other Titles in this Series

Howard Brenton
ANNE BOLEYN
BERLIN BERTIE
FAUST – PARTS ONE & TWO
    after Goethe
IN EXTREMIS
NEVER SO GOOD
PAUL
THE RAGGED TROUSERED
    PHILANTHROPISTS
    after Robert Tressell

Caryl Churchill
BLUE HEART
CHURCHILL PLAYS: THREE
CHURCHILL PLAYS: FOUR
CHURCHILL: SHORTS
CLOUD NINE
A DREAM PLAY *after* Strindberg
DRUNK ENOUGH TO SAY
    I LOVE YOU?
FAR AWAY
HOTEL
ICECREAM
LIGHT SHINING IN
    BUCKINGHAMSHIRE
MAD FOREST
A NUMBER
SEVEN JEWISH CHILDREN
THE SKRIKER
THIS IS A CHAIR
THYESTES *after* Seneca
TRAPS

Ariel Dorfman
DEATH AND THE MAIDEN
READER
THE RESISTANCE TRILOGY
WIDOWS

David Edgar
ALBERT SPEER
ARTHUR & GEORGE
CONTINENTAL DIVIDE
DR JEKYLL AND MR HYDE
    after Robert Louis Stephenson
EDGAR: SHORTS
PENTECOST
PLAYING WITH FIRE
THE PRISONER'S DILEMMA
THE SHAPE OF THE TABLE
TESTING THE ECHO
A TIME TO KEEP
    with Stephanie Dale

Debbie Tucker Green
BORN BAD
DIRTY BUTTERFLY
RANDOM
STONING MARY
TRADE & GENERATIONS

Ayub Khan-Din
EAST IS EAST
LAST DANCE AT DUM DUM
NOTES ON FALLING LEAVES
RAFTA, RAFTA...

Tony Kushner
ANGELS IN AMERICA –
    PARTS ONE & TWO
CAROLINE, OR CHANGE
HOMEBODY/KABUL

Liz Lochhead
BLOOD AND ICE
DRACULA *after* Bram Stoker
EDUCATING AGNES ('The School for
    Wives') *after* Molière
GOOD THINGS
MARY QUEEN OF SCOTS GOT HER
    HEAD CHOPPED OFF
MEDEA *after* Euripides
MISERYGUTS & TARTUFFE
    after Molière
PERFECT DAYS
THEBANS

Conor McPherson
DUBLIN CAROL
McPHERSON: FOUR PLAYS
McPHERSON PLAYS: TWO
PORT AUTHORITY
THE SEAFARER
SHINING CITY
THE WEIR

Arthur Miller
AN ENEMY OF THE PEOPLE
    after Ibsen
PLAYING FOR TIME

Enda Walsh
BEDBOUND & MISTERMAN
DELIRIUM
DISCO PIGS & SUCKING DUBLIN
THE NEW ELECTRIC BALLROOM
PENELOPE
THE SMALL THINGS
THE WALWORTH FARCE

Ariel Dorfman

PURGATORIO

NICK HERN BOOKS

London

www.nickhernbooks.co.uk

A Nick Hern Book

Purgatorio first published in Great Britain as an original paperback in 2006 by Nick Hern Books Limited, 14 Larden Road, London W3 7ST

Purgatorio and Afterword, copyright © 2006 Ariel Dorfman

Ariel Dorfman has asserted his right to be identified as the author of this work

Cover design by Ned Hoste, 2H

Typeset by Country Setting, Kingsdown, Kent CT14 8ES
Printed and bound in Great Britain by CLE Print Group Ltd, St Ives, Cambs PE27 3LE

A CIP catalogue record for this book is available from the British Library

ISBN   978 1 85459 669 7

For Angèlica

An earlier version of *Purgatorio* was first performed in a rehearsed reading at the Criterion Theatre, London, on 30 November 2001, with the following cast:

Juliet Stevenson
Simon Russell Beale

The first full production of the text printed here opened at the Seattle Repertory Theatre, Seattle, USA, on 2 November 2005, with the following cast:

Charlayne Woodard
Dan Snook

Director   David Esbjornson

Purgatorio received its UK premiere at the Arcola Theatre, London, on 15 January 2008, with the following cast:

Adjoa Andoh
Patrick Baladi

Director   Daniele Guerra
Set and Lighting Designer   Charles Edwards
Costumes   Jon Morrell

PURGATORIO

Characters

A MAN

A WOMAN

The play should be performed without an intermission.

A white room. Austere. No decorations. High up on the walls, a couple of slits let light filter in. A small bed, carefully made. A table. Two chairs. Reminds us of a room in an insane asylum or a prison where conjugal visits take place between inmates and their spouses. One door, with a small window, meshed with wire, through which somebody outside could look in. On the floor, against one of the walls, a small mirror.

In the room, a MAN *and a* WOMAN. *She is dressed in penitent colors. She has long hair, almost to her waist. He wears a doctor's white gown. The gown should be made of a light material so that when it is taken off, it feels like a second skin being peeled off easily. Glasses. A physician's bag next to him.*

MAN. So you want to escape. Good . . .

He takes a knife from the bag.

Here's the knife.

WOMAN. You said nobody was going to get hurt.

MAN. That depends on you, doesn't it? Pick up the knife. Pick it up.

She picks up the knife.

Good. Because it depends on you, doesn't it, if somebody gets hurt? Doesn't it?

WOMAN. Yes.

MAN. Well, well. Real progress.

WOMAN. I said the same thing to you yesterday.

MAN. That was a different yes. This yes came from the heart.

WOMAN. You can tell?

MAN. I've got that knack. I dabble in yeses. Aren't you lucky that I was assigned to you?

WOMAN. Yes!

MAN. Good! Now let's see if we can make some more progress today. Look what we have up there.

He points at a video camera on the fourth wall.

WOMAN. Tell me again how it works.

MAN. You've forgotten?

WOMAN. I like it when you explain it.

MAN. It's a camera. It films.

WOMAN. It films.

MAN. It takes images of you and me, of this room, of what we'll be doing and it captures those images, keeps them in there. Then, later, we can show the scene to anybody we want. We can repeat the scene over and over, as many times as we want. And they, the people in charge, can see what happened. That's why we're doing this. Remember? To show them. To prove it can be done.

WOMAN. To show them. To make them admire me again. So they understand who I am, what I could do again if I ever felt like it. To make them tremble.

MAN. Without hurting anyone.

The WOMAN *puts the knife down.*

WOMAN. I don't want to play anymore. I don't want things to get worse. For this to make things worse. If we're caught . . .

MAN. How can things get worse?

WOMAN. They could stop you from coming.

MAN. But not because you're trying to escape. You're supposed to try and escape. It gives you a flavour, a hankering for really leaving this place. It keeps you dreaming. I promise. Nobody will ever use that against you.

WOMAN. Not even if I break out? Creep down the corridor past the sleeping guards, make it to the floor below, get out the front door and –

MAN. And find yourself right back here, in this room, me and you and this knife.

WOMAN. And your promises.

MAN. And my promises.

WOMAN. You can promise all you want. How can you know? I mean, do you snore at night?

MAN. What do you mean?

WOMAN. At night. Do you snore?

MAN. I don't sleep, you know that.

WOMAN. Back then, before. When you were – did you snore at night?

MAN. No.

WOMAN. How do you know? How could you? Only the woman who slept at your side, only she would know if you snored or not.

MAN. The person I loved would have woken me up.

WOMAN. I didn't. He snored, my man – and I never woke him up, never told him. I would just watch him, listen in the dark first and then as it began to dawn, watch his lips moving ever so slightly, the breath and sound coming in and out of his body, dreaming of me. I'd draw his silhouette with my hands, like a shadow protecting him. Like the ointment I once spread all over his body. Rub, rub, rub, each piece of skin. Covering, protecting him with these hands. From far and then from near.

MAN. But you never woke him.

WOMAN. So he never knew. Just like you will never know. What they're planning, the people in charge. Or if you snore.

MAN. Unless the person I loved were to tell me someday. If I were to meet up with that person.

WOMAN. Is there a chance of that happening? You know how things are organised here. Has that ever happened, you know, a man and a woman who back then, before . . . ?

MAN. Never. It's against the rules.

WOMAN. The rules. The rules. I'm sick of these rules. I'm sick of this place.

MAN. You know what you have to do if you're really sick. Any time you're ready. But I mean really ready.

WOMAN. You know, back then, I mean, before, nobody ever guessed my plans, nobody ever knew what went on in my head. It was my one advantage. They never imagined that I could do what I did, not even in their nightmares. It was my one advantage over them.

MAN. Over him.

WOMAN. Yes. Over him too. And now these other people, the ones who send you here every day, every day, they know I'm a big risk, they watch me all the time.

MAN. They don't need to watch you. They're an Institution. The oldest one around. They have other things on their mind.

WOMAN. Like what?

MAN. Committee meetings. Things like that.

WOMAN. Well, I'm tired of them knowing everything about me, you knowing everything, when I don't –

MAN. Everything? I wouldn't say that. I wouldn't say we've come that far yet. There are lots of things you haven't told me.

WOMAN. You leave and I sit down on that bed and I think of what else, what I could have forgotten, but nothing comes, for years it seems nothing has come that's new. You've picked through my past as if it were a dead vulture. As if you were a vulture. There's nothing left. Not even the bones.

MAN. There is something left.

The WOMAN *refuses to answer, stubborn.*

All right. Let's go somewhere else. What if you were back there. On your island. If you could go back to your island.

The island you never saw again. Isn't there one thing you regret, one place . . . ?

WOMAN. Yes. On my island there's a bay where I'd – Not far from where I first saw him.

MAN. Your man.

WOMAN. This happened before he came, before he – I had a bad reputation. People said bad things about me. My father never listened to them. Maybe he should have. Maybe my brother should have. But they wouldn't hear a word against me.

MAN. They trusted you.

WOMAN. They trusted that girl, yes, the one who got up early in the mornings, before the dawn, to catch the sun coming up, to thank the sun, because the sun just gives and gives and never asks for anything in return. Only that we thank it, that we should be like it. This is something I never told you. A mile or so up the hill, just before you leave the last houses, there were some cats. Kittens, really. And when the first one saw me, he – or who knows if it wasn't a she, in cats it's hard to tell, even in humans we don't always really know – when this little thing, male or female, would see me, he'd start to mewl, almost caw, sweetly. And run towards me and when I kept on climbing – I was looking for berries and leaves and flowers, preparing brews in my head, that early in life, that early in the morning, what can heal, what can kill, what can make you dream, what can bring the dead back to life, what can make a man love a woman forever or close to forever, and just in case, just in case, what can burn the skin and set it on fire if it's inside a dress, and that blade in the foliage will do, yes, that yellow one, say its name or give it a name before using it – so I kept on climbing, and it would run ahead, the kitten. The poor thing thought I was bringing it some food, its milk.

MAN. How did they sound?

WOMAN. I'm not good at sounds.

MAN. I'd like to hear you try.

WOMAN. Meow, meow, meow, like that, calling. To someone
who had stopped coming, who had died or been sacrificed
to the gods or grown weary or sold into slavery – and they
thought I was that person. They'd almost but not quite rub
against my legs – and then, at some point, I'd leave them
behind, when I passed a cave on my right hand side. I guess
that was their hiding place, I guess that's when they realised
that I was not who they were waiting for, that I was not
going to bring them anything. Maybe then they knew that
the person who had fed them had died, his body hacked into
pieces and cast into the sea, was never coming back. Except
the next day when I climbed up that hill again – or maybe it
was two days later – they'd repeat the whole welcoming
ceremony all over again, overjoyed that I'd come, bearing
gifts. Only I wasn't. Each time I wasn't. Bearing gifts. By
then, my man had come, I had seen him and we had stood
in front of each other like two trees swaying to the same
wind and I knew he would take me far away, across the sea,
that I would open the kingdom to him, reveal its secrets and
how to conquer it.

MAN. Just as you had opened your heart to him?

WOMAN. Yes. I showed him who I was, I let him see
everything. Even what I would – So by then, I couldn't
be bothered with kittens and such. But that's my regret,
that's where I'd like to go. I'd like to bring them some milk,
maybe some warm bread. Baked by my own hands. My
own hands. See if they're still waiting for me. Imagine how
surprised they'll be, those tiny animals. Because then they'll
know they weren't wrong, I was the person they were
expecting. My soul, my gentle soul . . . I know what you're
thinking. You're thinking how could somebody like me –
these hands, these very hands –

MAN. And they'd be safe with you, the kittens?

WOMAN. I knew that's what you were going to ask.

MAN. You haven't answered my question. The kittens. Did
you ever think of hurting them?

The WOMAN *picks up the knife.*

WOMAN. What do the rules say about keeping the knife?

MAN. What did you feel, tell me what you felt when your man told you he was going to marry another woman, that girl. When he said he was doing it for you, for your boys. For your own good, he said.

Pause.

WOMAN. Did I tell you that?

MAN. How else would I know?

WOMAN. Then I don't need to tell you again.

MAN. You know, you're not being very cooperative today.

WOMAN. What if today turns out to be different?

MAN. Today doesn't seem very different so far. Am I missing something?

The WOMAN *puts down the knife.*

WOMAN. You know, that proverb you asked me to think about yesterday. The Chinese proverb.

MAN. If a woman opts for revenge . . .

WOMAN. . . . . she digs two graves. Yes, that one. I've been thinking about it. If a woman opts for revenge, she digs two graves. I've been thinking that maybe I did kill myself. That all the time I thought I was digging his grave I was also digging mine. That this is where I am now, in the grave I've dug for myself. And that he must be in another room with someone else tormenting him –

MAN. Is that what you think I'm doing? Tormenting you?

WOMAN. Someone like you tormenting him, that's what I've been thinking. That maybe I don't need to torment him from here. In my head. That I don't need to say to him in my head how much I hate him. Instead I can see him, hear him, imagine him, in the next room maybe, somewhere in this building, and he says to whoever it was his bad luck to draw as a visitor, someone just like you, I can hear him cry: Stop. Don't you think I've suffered enough?

MAN. That's a bit – overwrought, isn't it? Melodramatic? He doesn't sound like much of a man to me. Sounds like a crybaby. A whiner. Not at all how you've described him. What the legends say about him.

WOMAN. People like you can turn anybody into – you wear us down. You've probably worn him down.

MAN. So you imagine him saying, Enough, enough.

WOMAN. At some point, yes. He breaks. And that's when you –

MAN. Not me.

WOMAN. Someone like you, answers him, you . . . what does somebody like you answer him? Tell me that and maybe I can – Maybe it's what I need, just one more little push. To get him out of my system. That's what I've been thinking.

MAN. Even if I knew, I couldn't tell you that. It's against the rules.

WOMAN. Who will ever know? You said they're not watching. Go on. Indulge me. Tell me how you would react, how you would corner him, question him, if you were his visitor –

MAN. I'm not.

WOMAN. Just imagine you were in charge of him and he was standing in front of you and he said, Haven't I suffered enough?

MAN. All right. I'll play your game. Until the end – when the end comes, then it won't be a game anymore. And in any game, there are rules. Tell you what. Start me out. With the first thing you'd tell him. Give me that and I'll take it from there.

WOMAN. All right. You can never suffer enough.

MAN. That's it? What you'd say to him? You can never suffer enough.

WOMAN. Yes. Now it's your turn.

MAN. I'd say to him: You can never suffer enough. I'd say to him: Who's responsible? The woman who goes mad or the husband who drove her mad? You are the one, I'd say to him. You are the one who abandoned her.

WOMAN. Yes.

MAN. You are the one who said she was dangerous, said look what she did to her own father, to her own brother.

WOMAN. Things that I did for him.

MAN. Things that she did for you, I'd say to him, to save you, out of love for you.

WOMAN. Yes. And he smiled. Don't forget the smile.

MAN. You smiled, I'd say to him, you smiled, think of how she must have felt when you smiled at the thought that she would be thrown out on streets with her boys . . .

WOMAN. Streets we didn't recognise.

MAN. Without a language to defend herself and make herself known. Your own boys, I'd say to him, no place to go, no home left. She came to you . . .

WOMAN. I went down on my knees.

MAN. She went down on her knees. What she had never done ever before: down on her knees, and told you that she would have to beg from door to door the rest of her life, she who had been queen of the harvest, who had made the grains come out of the ground and . . . What else, what else?

WOMAN. I could have spent my life healing the scars in others if he had not taken me from my hearth and my father.

MAN. She begged you not to do this to her, to give her one more chance, just one more chance.

WOMAN. Give me one chance, one more chance, don't I deserve a few weeks to prove that I can change? Look at me. I'm on my knees. And he said: That's what knees are for, that's what a mouth is for. To his wife, the mother of his children: It's about time you learnt some humility.

MAN. Yes. That's what he said.

WOMAN. Yes. He asked me: Where are your mumbo-jumbo magic spells now? Where are your false snakes? He told me to find someone else, there are lots of men who'd like a piece of you. You're still a good fuck, he said. Do you want to have one last roll in bed before my wedding? No? Then go back, back, back to your father, he said, I'm sure he's planning a nice warm welcome after you hacked your brother into pieces and threw him on the waters. And then he said, my husband said: It's for your own good that I'm marrying. Come and meet her, my new bride. I'm sure you'll really like her. I'm sure you're going to be good friends. You could teach her some tricks in bed, you know, how to arch up that stiff pelvis of hers, give her some lessons.

MAN. And that's when you decided to fool him.

WOMAN. When he said I was going to be a good friend of his new wife. He gave me the idea.

MAN. You made him think you had repented. Changed.

WOMAN. He never really knew me.

MAN. You still love him.

WOMAN. No.

MAN. If you could only admit that you have kept on loving him . . .

WOMAN. I don't love him.

MAN. . . . then you might forgive him. Or even ask his forgiveness.

WOMAN. How would you know it was true?

MAN. We have ways. We have tests.

WOMAN. What sort of tests?

MAN. Words are never enough. Not if we want to send you back, if we want you to start over again pure, clean of your past. Purged.

WOMAN. If I repent, that is.

MAN. Everybody ends up doing it.

WOMAN. Everybody?

MAN. Almost everybody.

WOMAN. Have you ever thought – there's no solution to this one? To someone like me? There just isn't. No happy end to this one. Have you ever come up against a case where the only solution would be to eliminate, obliterate, I mean, finish that person off forever. Write her off. Write him off. No possible redemption.

MAN. We don't write anybody off. Not anybody. Not men, not women thousands of times worse than you.

WOMAN. Are there many of them?

MAN. Room after room after room. Like grains of sand at the bottom of an endless sea. Room after room, full, filling up fast, spilling over with women like you, men like him. Down there, things are getting – worse. Why should we give you special treatment?

WOMAN. Because I am special. He certainly thought so. Ask him. Ask whoever's assigned to him. Doing the same thing to him in the next room, sending him on his quest. So full of tasks, quests, missions. And now he's facing the most difficult of all: to forgive me. And I've been thinking, maybe I can beat him to it. I can forgive him before he forgives me. What you said: not to dig two graves.

MAN. And you are not just saying this to try and fool me like you fooled him? Like you fooled your father and your brother and everybody else? Even your children?

WOMAN. You said that you had other tests. Try me.

MAN. Are you telling me you're ready?

WOMAN. Have I ever said this to you before?

MAN. That doesn't mean you're ready.

WOMAN. Try me . . . Are you scared?

MAN. I don't want to fail.

WOMAN. That makes two of us. I don't want you to fail either.

MAN. You think this is a joke. But if you try and cheat, they'll withdraw me from your case, they will, they'll take you away from me.

WOMAN. Because the trust will have been broken, yes, yes, you told me all that. Would I risk losing you if – Why, you are scared of them.

MAN. No. I just don't think you've come far enough yet. You're tired, are just looking for an easy way out.

WOMAN. Would you say that to him? If he stood in front of you now and he said he'd had enough, enough, wanted to say how sorry he was, would you just dismiss him? Or would you give him a chance? The truth.

MAN. I'd give him a chance.

WOMAN. Because he's a man. Because you trust men to keep their word. But because I'm a woman . . . To refrain from imitation is the best revenge. You told me that. But now you don't think that a woman could –

MAN. You're not going to get away with this. You're going to ruin this for both of us. You don't know how rough this can be.

WOMAN. Oh, I'm quaking already. You really frighten me.

MAN. I'm warning you.

WOMAN. For my own good?

MAN. Yes. I do have your good in mind. That's what I'm supposed to do.

WOMAN. My own good. Don't you think I should decide what's good for me? Don't you think always having a man decide when a woman – ?

MAN. All right, all right. I know this is madness, I know you're not . . . Listen. Carefully. This is not going to work unless . . . You have to obey me. Do exactly what I ask.

WOMAN. Isn't that what I'm supposed to have learned from you? To be a good little girl so I can go back and enjoy life again?

MAN. What do you miss most?

WOMAN. The sex. What do you miss most?

MAN. I'm not allowed to speak about that.

WOMAN. Then it's bound to be sex.

MAN. You're not ready for this. I told you you weren't . . .

WOMAN. All right, all right. No more jokes. Look. Here I am. Obedient and ready.

MAN. You realise that now they will be watching, now it will all be recorded, official. If you fail me, they'll pull me off your case, I'll never come back. Someone else will, but – not me. You understand? Good. Now. First of all, you have to act as if I were your man.

WOMAN. So, this is a game?

MAN. No. I am him. Can you do that? See me as him?

WOMAN. You don't look at all like him, not a bit, but yes, I can do that. If that's what you need.

MAN. No. This is what you need. You need to make believe I am him. And you have to talk about our children.

WOMAN. Our children?

MAN. Our children. I'm him. Remember?

The MAN *switches on the camera.*

Now what I want to know, woman, is what was the worst part? That's what I need you to tell me. What you've always refused to talk about. When you saw the first drop of blood, knew you couldn't go back on what you . . . ? Was that the – ?

WOMAN. No. That wasn't the worst part.

MAN. Tell me.

WOMAN. I had ordered my slaves out of the room and locked the – this is very hard.

MAN. Maybe it was something he said, the eldest one. What did he say to you, the eldest one, your firstborn? He was first, right? Did I guess right?

WOMAN. Yes.

MAN. Why?

WOMAN. He was stronger than his little brother. It would have been – difficult to catch him, he would have run away, if he saw me, the eldest – if he had seen me . . .

MAN. Seen you what?

WOMAN. Doing what I . . . Doing that.

MAN. Not doing. Say it. Say it.

WOMAN. Killing.

MAN. No. Say it.

WOMAN. Murdering.

MAN. Good. Say it again.

WOMAN. If my firstborn had seen me murdering his little brother, it would have been more difficult to do the same thing to –

MAN. Say it. Use the words.

WOMAN. More difficult for me to murder him afterwards.

The MAN *is horrified but remains calm and in control.*

MAN. So you calculated. You were not insane. Your husband didn't drive you mad as you keep saying. You were fully aware. You had been planning that possibility since the children were born.

WOMAN. Since they were born. Before they were born. Since then. Maybe before we were born. Before anybody was born.

As the WOMAN *speaks, the lights begin to go down. As soon as we are in darkness, we hear the voice of the* MAN,

*surprisingly different, grunting, cheerful, counting. He will
continue to count up to any number which allows the
transition to happen.*

MAN. One. Two. Three. Four.

*Lights come up on the white room. Everything the same,
except the bed is not made and there is no knife. The* MAN
*does not have his white gown on, so his clothes and colors
look very similar to those the* WOMAN *wore before the
blackout. He no longer has glasses on and his hair seems
longer. He is on the floor, doing exercises: maybe pushups,
maybe abdominals. As he strains and puffs, he continues to
count his exertions, almost as if he were drilling.*

Five. Six. Seven.

The door opens. The WOMAN *enters. She has the doctor's
white gown on. And wears the slacks, turtleneck sweater,
shoes, that the* MAN *wore in the previous scene – and
glasses like his. Her formerly long hair is now tied up
neatly in a bun. She brings in the same large physician's
bag. She closes the door behind her. The* MAN *sees her but
continues doing his exercises.*

Wait. I've just got a few left. If you could – just – hold on –
until – I . . . And done.

*She nods, goes to the table, sits down, opens the bag,
extracts a notepad and begins to consult it. The* MAN
*finishes, stands up, goes over to her, panting. She hardly
looks at him, continues reading her notes.*

Sorry. I decided I might as well . . . You are late.

Pause. She continues to consult her notes.

I suppose that means your meeting was – I hope it means
you have news. Good news. They – what did they say?

WOMAN. Are you sure you're done? Finished? You don't
want to run around the room a few more times?

MAN. Why give us a body if we're not going to take care
of it?

WOMAN. The people in charge discovered that it keeps
    residents focused. Without a body of their own, they begin
    to forget who they are. But they didn't expect residents to
    start training for the marathon.

MAN. It's all an illusion anyway. What do they care what I do
    with my illusion?

Pause.

Except the verdict. There is a verdict, right?

WOMAN. They were moved by your final statement.
    Impressed is the word they suggested I convey to you. They
    thought it rang truthfully. Most of it.

MAN. Did they really say that? That it rang truthfully? And
    the tape, they must have liked the – ?

WOMAN. They saw it. Twice.

MAN. Twice! Do they do that for everybody? They must be
    busy, I mean, do they – ?

WOMAN. It's not always a good sign if they look at a tape
    twice, but in this case –

MAN. They've made their decision, given me the pass, go on,
    say it.

WOMAN. Well, they still have a few questions, just some
    minor quibbles really.

MAN. But they loved the tape, I knew they would. What else
    did they say?

WOMAN. They said . . . this man, he may well be the resident
    who's been in and out of here fastest – one of the people in
    charge who was at the meeting even let slip a comment, that
    if it went as well as expected, it might be a record.

MAN. A record! . . . Well, you should be proud. You're the one
    who did it. Maybe they'll commend you, give you – I don't
    know, do they give you bonuses for specially good work
    here, efficiency? Or do they – I mean, is there such a thing
    as a promotion?

WOMAN. I'm pretty far from a promotion, I'd say. Besides, you're the one who surprised them. They thought you were in for the long haul. Before you came in, they said so: 'It's going to take him an eternity. This one is going to be difficult.'

MAN. But I wasn't. After the first shock that is, I mean, when you came through that door and – I'm sorry I was unpleasant, but I'd been here for ages, just waiting, with only those women, those horrible, ugly women coming in and out once a day, never a word – I know, I know, I shouldn't care about how they look, but not even a smile –

WOMAN. They were impervious to your charms.

MAN. It was good for me, served me right. Got me in the mood to start work. I don't want to take any undue credit for this . . . record we've set, you and me, it's an honor of course, but I can't deny that I was prepared, I had a jump-start on everybody else. The fact that I killed myself, well, that has to have helped me.

WOMAN. I thought we had agreed it was a cowardly act.

MAN. It was. Of course it was. I admitted that the first time you brought it up, in our first session.

WOMAN. Second session.

MAN. You do remember everything. That's scary.

Pause.

But you have to accept that it did give me a boost in here, the fact that I had spent so much time brooding. Gave me an advantage, let's say. One thing I didn't mess up. Hanging myself, I mean . . . Do you have statistics about this sort of thing?

WOMAN. About hanging?

MAN. Statistics about suicide. Suicide and the rate of turnover, how fast it takes to get someone in and out of here, have you ever correlated the two?

WOMAN. Seems like a waste of time to me.

MAN. I don't know, it could help you plan. I mean, you must . . .
there has to be some sort of planning going on. This one got
rid of himself, he'll be out sooner, we can move this other
one into the room about to be vacated according to our
charts, that sort of thing. Here's this woman, she didn't
show signs of repenting back then, she'll take longer now.
Maybe it could help, you know. Control the inflow, outflow.
I mean, what happens if you run out of souls, don't have
enough to send back down there.

WOMAN. Are you trying to run this place? I thought you were
anxious to get out.

MAN. I can't wait. Just to be out there again, back where –
and before any of the – because the others are still here,
aren't they?

WOMAN. Who?

MAN. The people whose lives I shared, are they – ? I mean, if
I'm getting out the fastest, then they would have to still be
around, in a room like this one, I mean. I mean, they've
taken more time.

WOMAN. Her. That's who you're talking about, right? Her? If
she's already free?

MAN. Well, yes. Not because she'd repented, seen the light.
Not her. Not ever. It's just that she's so crafty. I thought
she'd certainly be out before me, before anyone. She fooled
me, that's for sure.

WOMAN. She's still here, believe me.

MAN. Who would have thought it? Still inside.

WOMAN. Do you like that? That someone's tormenting her?

MAN. No, in fact, I was hoping she'd . . . escaped. That she
was out there. I was hoping to meet her again. Find her
again.

WOMAN. Find her?

MAN. Other bodies, both of us, naturally. But I – there must
be some way we recognise each other, the other, look into

somebody's eyes. See what is in there, deeper than any deception or mask. Just like the first time we met and she told me what I was thinking, word for word. What you want, my boy, is to see my face underneath you while we make love, the one I haven't revealed to anyone. And then – beware. Once you see me, you won't forget me. I'm warning you. You will always recognise me, no matter what happens, no matter how much time passes. Once you've squeezed my face out from inside me, you will never be able to forget me. I'm warning you not to look unless you're ready to risk it.

WOMAN. Things women tell men.

The WOMAN *comes up to him, places her body next to his.*

Feel this.

MAN. You're asking me to – I can touch you? Is that allowed now that I'm – ?

The WOMAN *takes his hand and places it on her face, moves it down her neck to her shoulders, down to her hand.*

WOMAN. Just a husk. Nothing more. Not only now that we're here. The body is no more than an outer trapping. Clothes to be shed, even down there, even if you go deep into yourself. How she'll look, how you'll look, what sex, how old, what strands of hair and color of skin and softness of lip – none of it matters, none of it will help you one tiny little bit to know who anybody really is. How would you possibly recognise her?

The MAN *withdraws his hand. There is a pause.*

MAN. Have you ever been in love? Back then, down there? You're so – distant. As if there were no one at all inside you, no matter how much I look. Got rid of anyone you'd ever been, nothing left. So empty you – you don't seem to know anything about love, about what happens when two people . . . At times you have to break the other person open, dislodge them from who they used to be, let them shatter you as well. That's what we did: undress each other to the last bone. She had that capacity of looking through me, through everybody, like a knife.

WOMAN. Like a knife. A witch.

MAN. She wasn't really a witch. Just very . . . smart. She knew things about the earth, about people. She could see the future because she could see inside people.

WOMAN. But she didn't guess what you would do to her. So you're right. She wasn't much of a witch after all. Just knew the lay of that strange land.

Pause.

Maybe you'll be lucky enough not to meet her again next time.

MAN. Next time. Shouldn't we – you haven't told me anything about where I – do you have that information? Or maybe you're not allowed to give it to me.

WOMAN. Always in such a hurry. I thought I told you that we had a few questions left.

MAN. You said it was nothing serious, didn't you?

WOMAN. I'm not sure if that's how I put it. Discrepancies, let's say, holes, a minor contradiction or two. You wouldn't want to go on to the next stage unpurged, would you, tainted?

MAN. You said they loved the tape. So we'll clear up any discrepancy, whatever it might . . . and we'll – I'll be . . .

WOMAN. On your way, yes. Let's see. You stated, regarding your children: I loved those boys more than my own soul. But two days later, when we were seated here – come and sit with me here . . .

MAN. I'm afraid I didn't make the bed this morning.

WOMAN. Someone else will take care of that. Once you're out of here.

MAN. Do they change the sheets?

WOMAN. You want to tell us how to do our laundry now? Stop thinking about how to take over this whole operation and let's talk.

The WOMAN *pats the unmade bed. The* MAN *sits down next to her.*

So, two days later, let's see, yes, you state, here, read it.

MAN. What scared me in her was the same thing I loved in her. That she could do anything, was willing to try everything, defy every custom, break every rule, throw her home and family away, start all over with a man she hardly knew.

WOMAN. And that's also when you realised that if you uprooted her, betrayed her, there would be no stopping her, no rules would apply. Correct me if I'm misquoting you.

MAN. No, that's right. I understood she could do terrible things, go crazy, might do anything to me, to any children we might have.

WOMAN. Even kill them?

MAN. Yes. I said that to myself. If I leave her, dare to leave her. I saw it, the future. Saw it and then shut my eyes. And jumped. I thought, I can tame her. I can make her do whatever I want. She's so much in love that I can control everything, even her madness.

WOMAN. So you were planning to discard her someday, like a pair of old shoes, find a woman who spoke your own language, had your same skin, wasn't a savage, didn't make you afraid that she'd slit your throat some morning, from the beginning you had that plan? To set her aside when she was no longer useful. So. I want to know. That day you jumped – were your eyes open or were they closed?

MAN. Closed. They were closed. I already told you.

WOMAN. Open. They were open. You knew what was going to happen.

MAN. No.

WOMAN. Yes. You knew. Admit it. Eyes wide open. Admit it. You want to get out of here?

MAN. Yes. My eyes were – wide open.

WOMAN. Every step of the way. So it isn't true that you loved the boys more than your soul. You loved them less than your ambition, your pleasure. You sacrificed them, didn't you? Didn't you?

Pause.

What do I tell the people in charge? Who did you love more, yourself or the boys?

MAN (*low, hoarse voice*). Myself.

WOMAN. What?

MAN. Myself. I loved myself more.

WOMAN. And that's all you have to state about this incident?

MAN. Yes. My God. Are we done? Do you think the people in charge – is it enough? Will they accept it?

WOMAN. I'll try to convey your passion.

MAN. All they have to do is watch the tape – I mean, you're taping this, right?

WOMAN. Taping this?

MAN. Oh no, the camera's not on. You didn't tape it. Our last session, meeting, this goodbye, whatever you want to call this.

WOMAN. Why would we need a tape?

MAN (*sarcastically*). So you don't have to convey my passion. So I can plead my case by myself.

WOMAN. There's nothing to plead. They'll be satisfied with my report.

MAN. Well, that's a relief. So I'm going on. Good. So I go off now, right, to a new life as a little boy –

WOMAN. Or a little girl.

MAN. I wouldn't mind going back as a girl, not at all. You know that. We've discussed that. Whatever or whoever it is. As long as I get another stab at life.

WOMAN. Another stab at life?

MAN. I can't wait. Babies live the ultimate adventure. Everything new. Unnamed. Everything as if it were the first time. That first step. Then I'll fall down. No crying. I look up and see a hand, my mother's hand waiting to help me take my next step. I grab that hand, let it go, then fall down, scrape my knee, she picks me up, comforts me.

WOMAN. You seem awfully sure she's going to comfort you.

MAN. She's my mother.

Pause.

You wouldn't do that to me, give me a mother who . . .

WOMAN. Who what?

MAN. You wouldn't do that to me.

WOMAN. We're not doing anything to you. Not us.

Pause.

A mother who what?

MAN. When I am returned to – can I find myself back in – I mean, in time? I mean, you've always told me that time is not what we think it is, that it has a way of looping back, haunting you, repeating itself in strange ways, that things that seem to happen first are really happening later like in a Moebius strip, that's what I mean.

WOMAN. So?

MAN. Can I be sent back as . . .

WOMAN. As who? Who do you most fear being?

MAN. My son. One of my sons. I wouldn't want to be – put in his body, it wouldn't be fair to –

WOMAN. You don't think it would be fair to have the hand that picks you up be hers? Extremely fair for you to find yourself in that small body and watch her come up to you with a knife in her hand? This knife.

The WOMAN *takes a knife out of the bag.*

Do you recognise it? Would it be fair for those screams to be yours?

MAN. But what would you gain, what would I gain, anybody, by that? What would I learn, what – ?

WOMAN. I didn't say it was happening, you're the one who – But if that's what you think you deserve, if you had the idea . . .

The WOMAN *carefully puts the knife away in the bag.*

Maybe I should pass your suggestion along, maybe something can be arranged. Which of the two . . . ?

MAN. You don't – you people don't do things like that.

WOMAN. Are you scared?

MAN. You wouldn't do that. Nobody can go back as their own son.

WOMAN. Absolutely. That sort of thing doesn't happen. You're not here to be punished.

The MAN *gets down on his knees.*

MAN. I don't mind if next time I'm crippled or . . . poor . . . or anything like that. I deserve whatever –

WOMAN. Always debasing yourself. How did she ever fall in love with you, take you inside herself, this witch of yours? Why would she think someone like you was heroic, worth leaving her land for, killing her own children?

The MAN *stands up.*

MAN. She thought I was her equal, the most creative and adventurous man in the world. Someone who would change that world, build great cities, discover great inventions, cross frontiers, harness fire and wind, make the earth offer up its treasures. And she knew I needed her. To conquer the darkness, both of us, our names carved together into human memory. She trusted me. And I trusted her. Just one more mistake in a life full of mistakes.

WOMAN. Mistakes you never made?

MAN. What do you mean?

WOMAN. There's another question. It regards . . . this.

The WOMAN *takes a beautiful Grecian vase out of her bag.*

MAN. What's that?

WOMAN. Don't you recognise it? Your mother's favorite vase? The one you said you broke and then blamed it on your grandmother.

MAN. Oh, that vase.

WOMAN. Here. Read your statement about that incident.

MAN. I don't need to read any statement. We were at lunch, as usual. Alone, the two of us, my grandmother and me. I hated having to accompany her, hated my mother for forcing me to. Could you pass me that, pass me this, this that this that that. Just to bother me, to make me pay attention to the old woman. Till my grandmother asked me for one last thing, I can't remember what it . . . a napkin, maybe –

WOMAN. A piece of cheese. Here you say it was a piece of cheese.

MAN. Whatever it was, it was at her fingertips, all she had to do was move her finger an inch, less than an inch. I lunged across the table for it, angrily, no patience whatsoever, and broke the damn vase. And when my mother came in at the end of the meal, I blamed my grandmother. I swore she'd done it. And I liked it when my mother shouted at her, you stupid old woman. Stupid old woman. Years later I went into her room one last time, before I left on that journey – and crumbs were dribbling from her lips and her hand went out slowly, so slowly to the crumb and brought it to her mouth that trembled and it fell again and I tried to help her but she just stared past me as if I didn't exist and I saw she was going to die soon all by herself in that room and I felt a twinge of pity then, a hint of what I would feel later, now, when I think about her, that I never saw her again, never told her I was sorry.

WOMAN. Except that there's nothing to be sorry for. Your grandmother says that she's the one who broke it. Here it is, part of her statement: I can't forgive myself for having let that child be punished for something I did. I wish I could see him again to thank him for being so sweet, defending me when I had no one else in the world who cared.

MAN. I'm the one who broke the damn thing. And the fact that she's trying to clear me of blame, makes what I did even worse.

WOMAN. We don't think so. We think she's right. In fact we're sure she's right. You covered up something good you'd done, covered up your tenderness as if it were an embarrassment. Why?

MAN. What do you want me to answer if that's how I remember it? I can see my arm stabbing across the table, enraged, the vase shattering at her feet, deciding, coldly, deliberately, to blame my grandmother.

WOMAN. So how do you explain . . . ?

MAN. Maybe I was – I confused that incident with another one. I know I broke a vase when I was younger, maybe I confused the two vases.

The WOMAN *stands up, opens the bag as if getting ready to leave.*

WOMAN. I'll tell them you refuse to cooperate.

MAN. Wait! Maybe . . .

WOMAN. Maybe?

MAN. Maybe – I wanted to please you. Something else, you said. One more thing. One more piece of meat. One more juicy item. We need to convince them. I need more. Shock me. I'm done. I told you I was done. But you wanted me to make myself small like an insect so I could start again and you could get – what, a promotion, a bonus, a congratulation, a what? Attention, attention. My resident is clean. Cleaned out. Stainless, washed, scrubbed. Repented of every last ultimate penultimate final sin, mistake, oversight, error, transgression, every ant he crushed and toe he stepped on. So maybe . . .

WOMAN. Maybe . . .

MAN. I'd sit here for hours, running or doing my exercises, pushing the walls, pushing the door, pushing the floor, jumping, jumping, trying to think of how to give you what you needed. Maybe something broke inside me, broke down, something snapped and maybe I – one day I – I may have started to invent things. But it was only that one time, with my grandmother. That's all. Just that one time. Can't we just forget it?

WOMAN. What if it wasn't just that one time? What if it was . . . all the time? What they suspect.

MAN. You told me they were impressed. You told me I was the fastest, that they're sending me off.

WOMAN. Always in such a rush. You're forgetting one more piece of the puzzle. Your suicide.

MAN. I thought that was a point in my favour, to arrive already remorseful.

WOMAN. It is, it certainly is. But it also alerts us. We know what it's like, the wrenching madness of that moment when your body is peeled away from you, like a screech. You thought it was ending, you were on the verge of ridding yourself of those voices, those screams of your sons, the eyes of that witch.

MAN. Yes. That's what I prayed for.

WOMAN. But you didn't. End it, I mean. You opened your eyes and here you were, in this room, with only your shrivelled self for infinity and a day, and no distractions. No more quests or adventures, no more drinking or drums. Just yourself and some ugly guards and me. And that's when you made your mistake. You submitted to me right away.

MAN. Not right away. The second session. After a night of thought I –

WOMAN. It was too quick. It happens all the time. First day, you resist, you keep up the pretence of your wounded dignity, deny you ever did a thing. Then I leave and you're alone. A night passes and then another and I don't come back. And you think to yourself at some point during the third sleepless night, I'm going to confess anyway, sooner or later, they hold all the cards, why not do it right away, beat the others to it, save myself the trouble? Wasn't that what happened?

MAN. No.

WOMAN. Wasn't that what happened? You planned everything. Isn't that who you are, a man of action who, once he figures out how to beat the enemy, maps out a strategy and then sticks to it? Always you, the same you, dancing on the edge of your own cliff, always sure you wouldn't fall. Giving what you thought was the best performance of any of your existences. Didn't you try to cheat us, cheat me? Take a shortcut, not do all the work? Say it. Aren't you tired of lying all the time?

Pause.

Don't you want this over?

MAN. I wanted to cheat you. That's who I am, who I was, someone who's impatient, always on his way somewhere else. But that doesn't mean it wasn't true, that it didn't turn into something true over time, that journey into the swamp of myself. When a man opts for revenge, he digs two graves. You gave me those words. And I thought about my wife. And as I came closer to her, I began to miss her, hoped that maybe in our next life span, even if I don't recognise it or realise it, even if I go back as a woman, she would come up to me again and tell me my most secret thoughts, that moment when we were like two trees banishing our fears under the same wind. Or maybe enough just to sleep by her side one more time, be awoken by her again in the night.

WOMAN. She had nightmares.

MAN. No, it wasn't nightmares that woke me up. Just that she snored slightly, I don't think I ever told you about this?

WOMAN. Not a word.

MAN. I wouldn't stir, stayed quietly next to her, imagining her secret dreams, the spells she was casting in her dreams. Listen in the dark first and then, as it began to dawn, watch her lips moving ever so slightly, like the breeze on a field of black wheat, up and down, tinkling the grapes, preparing them to be wine, the breath and sound coming in and out of her body. I'd fly my hands over her body, like a shadow protecting her. Thinking this love was forever. That her body could never be apart from mine. Never thinking that I could ever want anyone else breathing, echoing secretly near to me. I'm ready to find her again, help her to heal, I can't possibly be more ready.

WOMAN. Now that you've been stripped of your last illusion about yourself, now that you have come as far as you can possibly go by yourself . . .

The WOMAN *goes to the door.*

The next stage is waiting for you.

Pause.

Do you know what's on the other side of the door, of the light? What's out there?

MAN. A new birth. A life like a beach, you said, that nobody has ever stepped on, clean as the first day of creation.

WOMAN. No. Something else.

MAN. What else could it be?

WOMAN. Not what. Who. She's there. In a room. Just like this one. The next room, in fact. Where she's waiting for you. The next stage.

MAN. She – she's been waiting for me all these years?

WOMAN. For her, no time has passed. That's how things are here. For your wife, when you walk through that door, her door, as far as she's concerned, she died yesterday, the day before yesterday.

MAN. So she's not ready to go back?

WOMAN. She's fresh, just starting. As angry and unrelenting as when she died.

MAN. What do I have to do?

WOMAN. Not you. Her. She has to repent.

MAN. And I have to get her there.

WOMAN. Like I did with you.

MAN. And she will never know who I am?

WOMAN. You can't tell her. Not ever. The moment you even drop a hint, you'll find yourself back here with someone like me. Going through it all again. Starting all over.

MAN. You people – you people, you're – you're just playing with me. A game, all a game for – what? Your entertainment? Their entertainment?

WOMAN. Not a game. Believe me, it's not a –

MAN. You lied to me. From the start. When you said: You're the one who – To refrain from imitation is the best revenge, you said. A lie. You people are seeking revenge.

WOMAN. Not revenge. A chance at redemption. Healing her while you heal yourself.

MAN. I can't do it!

WOMAN. I learned. Everybody does it. Think of it as another quest. The greatest quest of all.

MAN. I can't do it!!

The MAN *turns violently, accidentally hits the vase. It falls and shatters.*

I'm sorry, I –

WOMAN. No, it was my fault, I shouldn't have left it there when –

The MAN *gets down on his hands and knees and starts to pick up the pieces.*

It will be picked up once you're gone, once you –

She gets down on her hands and knees and helps him pick up the pieces. They put the pieces in the bag. They stand up.

MAN. It's . . . going to take a long time. To get her to . . . cooperate.

WOMAN. I know.

MAN. It'll take forever.

WOMAN. Yes. But that's what you've got, after all, as of now.

The MAN *opens the door. He stops, looks at the* WOMAN.

MAN. There's just one thing I need to know. Does the circle ever close?

WOMAN. If you can heal her, yes.

The MAN *leaves and closes the door behind him. The* WOMAN *is left alone. She takes in the emptiness of the room and her own solitude.*

If you can heal her, yes.

There is a blackout. We hear the voice of the MAN.

MAN (*off*). Now what I want to know, woman, is what was the worst part? That's what I need you to tell me. What you've always refused to talk about.

When the lights rise, we are back at the spot and time when the interrogation started a few minutes before the previous blackout, the MAN *and the* WOMAN *as before, in the same positions they occupied. He as the Healer with white gown and glasses, and she again as the Resident. That scene will now be repeated.*

When you saw the first drop of blood, knew you couldn't go back on what you . . . ? Was that the – ?

WOMAN. No. That wasn't the worst part.

MAN. Tell me.

WOMAN. I had ordered my slaves out of the room and locked the – This is very hard.

MAN. Maybe it was something he said, the eldest one. What did he say to you, the eldest one, your firstborn? He was first, right? Did I guess right?

WOMAN. Yes.

MAN. Why?

WOMAN. He was stronger than his little brother. It would have been – difficult to catch him, he would have run away, if he saw me, the eldest – if he had seen me . . .

MAN. Seen you what?

WOMAN. Doing what I . . . Doing that.

MAN. Not doing. Say it. Say it.

WOMAN. Killing.

MAN. No. Say it.

WOMAN. Murdering.

MAN. Good. Say it again.

WOMAN. If my firstborn had seen me murdering his little brother, it would have been more difficult to do the same thing to –

MAN. Say it. Use the words.

WOMAN. More difficult for me to murder him afterwards.

The MAN *is horrified but remains calm and in control.*

MAN. So you calculated. You were not insane. Your husband didn't drive you mad as you keep saying. You were fully aware. You had been planning that possibility since the children were born.

WOMAN. Since they were born. Before they were born. Since then. Maybe before we were born. Before anybody was born.

MAN. Forget anybody else. Tell me about that moment. The crime you meditated carefully, each stage. You chose the strongest first, because the little one could then do nothing? He would be defenceless whereas your eldest son would have resisted? You knew exactly what you were doing. Is that what you're saying to me?

WOMAN. You asked me about the worst part. That was it.

MAN. Planning it, planning it?

WOMAN. No. The look in his eyes, the look in the eyes of my baby, the little one. When he saw what I was doing to his brother, that look when the first blood splattered my hands and face and he understood it was not a game. He knew.

MAN. What did he know?

WOMAN. That he was next. That when I had done with his brother, I would start with him. With the same knife. That he would not even get a clean knife. It took me five minutes. My eldest boy took five minutes to die. And the other one watched with me –

MAN. Tell me his name.

WOMAN. No! Not his name. I will never tell you his name. He watched me, the little one, while his brother died. That's what I can't forgive myself for.

MAN. Good. Good.

WOMAN. For those five minutes when he knew.

MAN. What did he say to you? Did he try to run away, the little one?

WOMAN. He just stood there. Watching. And when I was done, once I had kissed his dead brother one last time and let him fall gently to the ground, let him slip out of my arms one last time as if I were putting him to bed, when I turned to him, to the little one who was staring at me from across the room, while outside they were shouting, they were trying to break down the door, my husband was screaming at them to hurry, to hurry –

MAN. And you enjoyed hearing him scream?

WOMAN. I suppose so. It's what I wanted back then. I wanted to hear his screams, for him to hear the screams of his son, not even knowing which of them was dying first. Now I'm sorry for him, for my husband.

MAN. He can't stop hearing those screams.

WOMAN. Yes. Inside. Those screams, over and over. He knows that you pay for what you do. That you can't just go through life making promises and hurting and plundering other lives and never never pay. But – enough.

MAN. You think he's suffered enough. You're ready to forgive him.

WOMAN. He's not what really matters. I wasn't really listening to him back then, if you want to know the truth. I had turned to my baby. He came to me. He didn't run away. He came up to me and took the free hand. It was covered with blood, but he took it anyway, in both his hands. He looked down at his brother, then up at me. And then he spoke. It was suddenly very quiet. The pounding outside, the shouts, had stopped. As if my husband were also listening.

MAN. And the little one, what did he say?

WOMAN. Mother. Please, mother. Like this. In a whisper. Only that. Mother. Please, mother. I wanted to spare him. If I could have brought his brother back to life right then, I would have. But it was too late. There was a time when I was a girl when . . . But now it was too late. I had lost my powers. I had crossed the seas, gone West, no longer used the language I had been born into, and my powers had . . . And then my husband started to batter on the door again. So I did it.

MAN. And your eyes were open?

WOMAN. I owed it to him, my second-born, my baby. The one who looked most like his father. That he should see my eyes and be less scared while I – I'm so sorry. I'm so . . .

MAN. Kneel. On your knees.

The WOMAN *slowly gets down on one knee.*

Both knees. Good. Now go on. Remember. I am him. I am your husband. Say it to me. Looking at me. Looking at me, I said.

WOMAN (*almost inaudible*). I want him . . . I want him to forgive me.

MAN. I need to hear your voice. We both need to hear it.

WOMAN. I want him to forgive me. To see him one more time so he can forgive me.

MAN. Good. That's the way. What about her?

WOMAN. Her?

MAN. Look at me. Good. Yes, I want to see your eyes. What about the other woman, the young lovely innocent girl your husband was leaving you for? Are you sorry for her? That you took her life, poisoned her skin with fire, wrapped her in death as if she were a whore, burnt her down to her bones, the same look in her eyes as in the eyes of your little one, knowing she was going to die. Are you sorry for her?

WOMAN. Yes.

MAN. Say it. Look at me. Say it.

WOMAN. I should never have done it. I was crazy with jealousy.

MAN. Not crazy. You knew what you were doing.

WOMAN. Angry. Angry that they were casting me out, that I should spend my night on the seas looking for a home, vomiting while she was making love with my man, while she was making him groan with pleasure. Oh, it still hurts me. He still hurts me.

MAN. So you still love him?

WOMAN. No.

MAN. The truth. I am your man. Your husband. You can say it to me. Do you still love me?

She hesitates, finally, painfully, answers.

WOMAN. Yes.

MAN. Good. Now we're ready. Now you can ask for forgiveness. Ask me, go on.

WOMAN. I'm sorry I killed our boys.

MAN. No. Her. Ask me to forgive you for her, for having killed my bride, a sweeter love than you ever were. Younger

than you. With skin light like mine. Who spoke my own
language. Not a foreigner like you.

The WOMAN *stands up.*

WOMAN. Don't say that.

MAN. Not a savage like you. Someone who knew how to read,
how to write, how to play music. A better woman than you
will ever be.

WOMAN. Don't say that. Not that. He would never have said
that.

MAN. How do you know? What if that is what your husband
was thinking, still thinks, deep inside himself, lost
somewhere in this building? Could you still forgive him?
Do you still love him enough? Say it, say it. We are trying
to heal you, remember? Testing you, remember? Say that
you forgive him, beg for his forgiveness.

WOMAN. No.

They both stay like that for a while, wordless.

MAN. What about the children? Are you sorry about them? Or
was that also a sham?

WOMAN. I would do it again. He was going to take them
from me, bring them up to hate the witch, laugh at me in
my old age when I came to their door crippled, with my
hands out asking for a crust of bread while he bragged out
stories to my boys about the bitter woman who had
accidentally given them birth, the bitch who couldn't be
trusted because she betrayed her own father and her own
fatherland, the barbarian bitch who never fully learned the
language of her husband's land. What was I to do? Are they
always going to get away with it? Are they always going to
win? Only his story to be told, like an echo in the ears and
alphabet of others. First he crossed the sea, then he asked
me to give him the secrets and the maps and the hidden
words that would open the legs of the land to him. Force the
legs of the land open for him. Who reproaches a warrior
like him, a man who slays the dragons? A man who
ransacks the land, lays waste to the cities, burns them to the

ground and then is remembered in statues and legends and name places. The hero. The one who tells the stories and exults by the fire while girls undress for his eyes only. And me? What about me? I would be remembered, forever and ever, as exile, fool, deceived lover, abandoned by the Gods and abandoned by her man, sorceress, slut, traitor, the woman who opened the door to the enemy.

MAN. Sorceress, slut, traitor – that's how you deserve to be remembered. A woman who killed her children and didn't let their father say goodbye, didn't even give him the bodies for burial.

WOMAN. I gave them life.

MAN. Life?!

WOMAN. I split myself open to give them life. I carried them. My sex. And my body. And my breasts. Mine. My milk. Oh my babies, my babies. Oh if I could go back to the day my mother gave me life, my father and my mother – burn the bed, knife my mother before she gave birth to me. Back to the beginning of everything, everything and burn it down, before anybody could ever be born.

MAN. That's your answer? Destroy and kill and burn? . . . You know what I'm going to do? I'm going to have them send you back. Just as you are now. Send you back . . . in her body.

WOMAN. In her body?

MAN. Yes, your mind in her body. That girl. Her. The bride you set on fire so your man could never touch her like he'd touched you, sigh the same things to her in the night. You don't feel sorry for her? Not even a bit?

WOMAN. I'm only sorry it did not last longer. She died too quickly, that's my only regret.

MAN. So it'll do you good to know her from inside. That young woman who stole him away from you. Isn't that what you most fear? Isn't that what you need – to tame you a bit, make you humble, soften you up, so next time you come into this room, you'll bow your head, submit, really seek to

heal yourself? Yes, yes, that's what I'll recommend they do
to you.

WOMAN. You'd do that to me?

MAN. And enjoy every minute of it, watching you from here,
watching as you make love to your man inside the body of
another woman, wait for the fire to burn you through and
through, purge you so you can understand . . . So you have
to start again . . . Oh, I'll enjoy it.

The WOMAN *reacts violently, pushing the* MAN *toward
the door. He resists her fury.*

WOMAN. Out, out, get out. Out, you bastard.

The MAN *forces her back to the bed and pins her down.*

MAN. I'll leave. I'll leave when I want to, when I'm good and
ready. I go and I come as I please. And can do what I want
with you. We own you. Like the slaves you used to own.

WOMAN. You don't own me. Not until I give you what you
want. Not until I repent. But let me tell you something. If
I do repent, it's not me. I would have to stop being myself.
Whoever it is that repents tomorrow or the next day or a
million years from now, it's not me, do you understand?
I want you to remember this. Hey. You there. You people
who are filming this with your stupid cameras. Listen to
me, stuff me into your eyes and ears. The woman who says
those words, kneels in front of you and you and you and
says those words, that I'm sorry, I'm sorry I killed the
whore who stole my man, that woman who confesses on her
knees will be someone else. Not me. Remember that
tomorrow.

MAN. Tomorrow? Well, it's not going to be me tomorrow. Not
me.

WOMAN. It will be you. You, back for more. In another body,
who knows what body they'll choose for you. But still you,
inside him, inside her. You.

MAN. No. Not me.

WOMAN. When I pushed you, tried to push you out that door,
you fought back. You fought to stay here. You wanted to

stay here! Every muscle in your body was straining to stay. I'm your case. Your only case. When I go back, you go back. When I'm erased, they erase you too. Right? Am I right? Isn't that your mission?

MAN (*passionate*). I wanted to heal you. I still want to heal you.

WOMAN (*just as passionate*). No. It's something else. Why don't you ever give up? I need the truth. Just like I told it to you, my truth. How it still hurts me. That I still love him. For once, the truth. Just this once. Even if you risk everything, everything, lose everything, by telling me. What keeps you coming back?

MAN. You. I come back because of you. Because of that look in your son's eyes as he watched. We can erase it. Forget it. Together. Never have to remember it ever again. Start all over. You and me. The warm waters of peace. The warm waters of forgiveness. The warm waters of not being yourself.

She looks deep into him.

WOMAN. You're him. It's you, isn't it?

A long pause.

MAN. Yes.

The MAN *takes off his glasses. Takes off his white gown. He is now just like her, both of them clad in penitent black.*

Incredibly long pause.

WOMAN. It's going to take forever.

MAN. I have nowhere else to go.

They look at each other silently, as lights go down. They are bathed in a pool of light excluding everything but the MAN *and the* WOMAN. *The light slowly fades, leaving them glowing nakedly in the dark.*

Afterword

Purgatorio started, like so many of my plays and novels, with an image, an image that came to me without warning and then stubbornly would not go away.

Appropriately, the place where this visitation transpired was Cadaqués, the seaside town in Cataluña where my wife and I had sought refuge for a month. One morning, on the last day of our sojourn, not far from where Dalí and Gala had found love, and the ghosts of García Lorca and Eluard, Miró and Buñuel and Magritte still roam, that last morning, as if those dead artists were whispering to me from some purgatorial universe of their own, I awoke with a vision.

There they were, a man and a woman in an austere room – it could be an insane asylum, a hospital, perhaps something more dire – and she wanted to escape and he held the key and wished to help her but there was also something in the man that was full of rage, something that he was concealing.

I didn't, of course, know who they were. And the only way to find out was to set them free in my imagination, let them talk, jab at each other until they would be forced to reveal themselves. It was only after they beat around the bush of each other for a while that it began to dawn upon me what sort of space they might be inhabiting: that man and that woman were residents of the afterlife. Not strange that I had reached such a conclusion about their condition. What happens to the dead and how they speak to us has always been, since I was a child, one of my obsessions.*

---

* An obsession which still haunts me now, years after I completed *Purgatorio*. My last four poems have given a voice to Columbus, Picasso, William Blake, Hammurabi, as if they were dictating those words to me from beyond the grave, possessing my tongue to caution readers about our current blindness, cruelty and folly.

I automatically called that place Purgatorio, though I was later to realize that I had conceived the hereafter as more Buddhist than Christian, less an orderly Dantesque circle in the sky than a claustrophobic dreamscape outside ordinary time and space where anything is possible.

But who were they, that man, that woman, what did they want from each other?

For a long time, I had been wondering about the terrible things we humans do to one another and how – indeed if – there can be some sort of reparation, some trace of redemption. I had explored these themes, of course, in some of my other plays, *Death and the Maiden*, *Widows* and *Reader*, but was eager to delve into these issues in an arena less overtly political. What would happen if, instead of an agent of the state executing or torturing or censuring victims or hiding bodies, I brought together on stage one woman and one man who had damaged one another irreparably? Because it always comes down to one human being facing another one, always starts there, one on one, in the theatre and in life, it always starts there.

What was essential, I thought, was to refrain from making one antagonist good and the other bad, avoid the temptation to enunciate an easy answer. I wanted both characters to simultaneously interrogate and heal each other, be the therapist for the other's liberation and also the possible means to his or her damnation, both of them the coincident guardians of heaven and hell. The aesthetic challenge was to find a way to create a twist in theatrical time where such a switch of identities would not feel artificial, allowing me to play with the audience in the same way that each of my protagonists plays with the other, hides from him, from her, from their own selves. From the very beginning, I knew these two were performing for each other. In a sense, I wanted to discover whether they (or anyone, for that matter) can go beyond the mask of performance and see deep into the soul of the other, that which is not mere acting-for-the-other. The double (multiple) interrogation/trial is a way of breaking down the personality of the players, ripping off the veils of their ego. Playing, all of us, hide-and-seek as a roundabout way of fully registering, perhaps testing, our humanity.

A playfulness made more urgent by the magnitude of the dilemmas I was posing on stage. *Purgatorio*, in fact, can be seen as an emotional and intellectual sequel to *Death and the Maiden*, exploring further some of the questions opened up by Paulina Salas in that first play of mine, trying to go beyond those questions: Can there be forgiveness and reconciliation if we have committed monstrous deeds? How can we be expected to repent of those deeds without destroying our own identity, the bedrock of our past, the very actions yesterday which turned us into who we are today? And what if repentance is not enough? After all, how do we know if someone is really ready to atone or is only faking it? And what if the one person who holds the key to my redemption happens to be the person I have most hurt in this world?

It was this last question that I was most interested in exploring, because it might provide, I thought, the key to the identity of the characters. As I began to accompany that man and that woman on their journey, I pondered why they were withholding their past not only from each other but also from me, what unforgivable crimes they could have committed against each other. What is the worse thing a woman can do to a man? And a man to a woman?

And gradually, it came to me, I extracted the secret of their remorse, who they might have been when alive, who they were now: Jason and Medea, I said to myself, that's who, caught in Purgatory, each holding out the promise of oblivion to the other, the promise of salvation, the threat of eternal torment and interrogation. But not only those two mythical figures whom I had been circling like a hunter for decades, not only a way to innovatively, maybe fruitfully, engage the classics in our time. That story also resonated with the echoes of other warriors who have always ventured forth on voyages of conquest and echoes of the native women who have awaited them on the far shore. I conjured up as well a conqueror like Cortés and his lover and translator, La Malinche; I wanted to evoke the multiple carnal and intellectual meetings which, full of cunning and sex and enthralment with the exotic foreigner, have peopled history, have given birth, like dragon teeth springing from the ground, to the children of our contemporary world.

So I let them tear into each other, my protagonists, let them try to reach a reconciliation, figure out how to absolve what they had perpetrated or perhaps discover that there is no solution, no way out of the maze, that this is what tragedy in our times means.

Because, finally, even if *Purgatorio* deals with a man and a woman who came to life and words thousands of years ago, it is foremost a story for our era and, more specifically, marked by the aftermath of 9/11. (Politics again, creeping onto the stage through the back door!) This play asks us how we should react when we have been devastated by some intolerable offence, dares us to question our own assumptions about reality, reveals how easy it is to go from victim to accuser, from victim to invader, from violator to victim. And it was my hope that, at a time when our planet and our species face tremendous problems of guilt and carnage, when horror done to us yesterday invites terror that we inflict on others tomorrow, it was my hope that the play could at least pose the question of how to venture beyond the cycle of blame and anger.

Whether such deliverance was feasible did not depend, I knew, on my hopes, my plans, even my talents. It was up to that man and that woman in that room, and up to the men and women watching them from the larger, replicating rooms of each theatre: they are the ones who will decide whether we are to be damned or redeemed.

Determine if we are one day to break out of the cycle of hatred and retribution.

Because *Purgatorio,* ultimately, is about trust.

Can anything be more urgent than to find a way of trusting one another, trusting our improbable enemy, the loved one who has hurt us, the beloved we have hurt, can anything be more urgent in this world of ours contaminated by violence and fear and betrayal?

August 2006

Acknowledgements

I believe I can speak for the man and the woman in that room when I offer thanks to those who helped bring them to the stage so they could thrash out in the afterlife what they were unable to resolve while alive. It goes without saying that this play owes more than I can briefly express here to David Esbjornson, Charlayne Woodard, Dan Snook, as well as to my son, Rodrigo, who was its dramaturge, almost its midwife, all of whom, along with the many artists and staff of the Seattle Rep worked tirelessly to help me transmit my vision. Thanks to Priscilla Lopez and Tom Hewitt who participated with passion and intelligence in a ten day workshop at Duke University, organized by indefatigable Zannie Voss; and to Juliet Stevenson and Simon Russell Beale, who first read the play publicly in London. Wilson Milam was a loyal collaborator and friend and never lost his faith in the play. Crucial, also, were two producers of *Purgatorio*: the glorious Benjamin Mordecai, who did not live to see on stage the work he so fervently believed in; and Clare Lawrence, who never flagged in her efforts to bring it to a London audience. Thanks also to my devoted agents, Peter Hagan, Catherine Anderson and Julia Tyrrell. I am, in addition, grateful to my tenacious and dedicated editor, Nick Hern, and to Alessandra Serra and Uwe Carstenson, wonderful translators of the play into Italian and German respectively. Finally, if *Purgatorio* is dedicated to Angélica, my wife and *compañera* of so many years, it is because without her neither the play nor its author would have survived.